CW01116737

TO: ———————————

FROM: ———————————

This compilation copyright © 1995 Lion Publishing
Illustrations copyright © 1995 Susan Pontefract
Published by
Lion Publishing plc
Sandy Lane West, Oxford, England
ISBN 0 7459 3363 7
Albatross Books Pty Ltd
PO Box 320, Sutherland, NSW 2232, Australia
ISBN 0 7324 1325 7

First edition 1995
10 9 8 7 6 5 4 3 2 1 0

All rights reserved

Acknowledgments
Illustrations: Susan Pontefract
'God Gives You This Day' © copyright Stewart
Henderson from the collection *A Giant's Scrapbook*
published by Hodder and Stoughton;
'Love Song' copyright © Cathy Anderson

A catalogue record for this book is available
from the British Library

Printed and bound in Singapore

LOVE POETRY
— *across the* —
CENTURIES

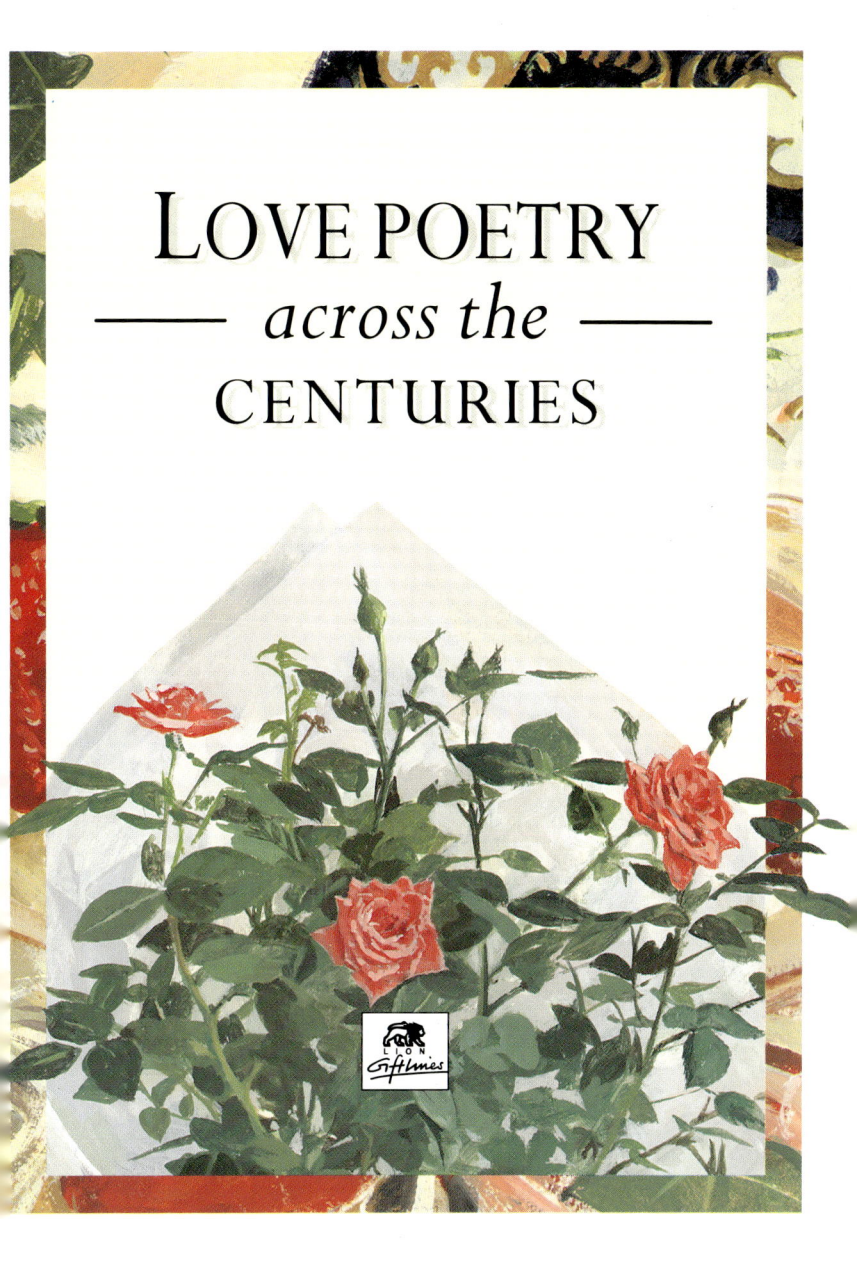

Susan Pontefract's paintings are inspired by the rich imagery of the Song of Songs:

There among blossom and vine
   I will give you my love,
Musk of the violet mandrakes
   spilled upon us . . .
And returning, finding our doorways
   piled with fruits,
The best of the new-picked
   and the long-stored,
My love, I will give you
   all I have saved for you.

Contents

LOVE'S BIRTH
12

WEDDING DAY
14

BEING TOGETHER
16

LOVE'S PASSION
18

LOVE'S FIDELITY
20

COMPANIONSHIP
22

LOVE'S GIVING
24

LOVE AND TIME
26

BLESSINGS
28

There are four things that are too mysterious
for me to understand:
an eagle flying in the sky,
a snake moving on a rock,
a ship finding its way over the sea,
and a man and a woman falling in love.

From the book of Proverbs

INTRODUCTION

From earliest times men and women have expressed their love for each other through poetry. This anthology includes ancient love poetry from the Bible and a selection of classic and contemporary poems. Together they represent a human response to the divine gift of love and loving—making this book a gift which will express something of the experience of those who love.

At the heart of the Bible is one of the most beautiful love poems ever written—the Song of Songs. It celebrates human love and sexuality as a gift from God. The Bible has a great deal to say about love—God's love for us and ours for God—but also about this human love for each other. The passages from the Bible included in this collection demonstrate with insight and beauty the place of love at the heart of our world.

LOVE'S BIRTH

My beloved speaks and says to me:
'Arise, my love, my fair one,
and come away;
for now the winter is past,
the rain is over and gone.
The flowers appear on the earth;
the time of singing has come
and the voice of the turtledove
is heard in our land.
The fig tree puts forth its figs,
and the vines are in blossom;
they give forth fragrance.
Arise, my love, my fair one,
and come away.'

From the Song of Songs

A Birthday

My heart is like a singing bird
    Whose nest is in a watered shoot;
My heart is like an apple-tree
    Whose boughs are bent with thick-set fruit;
My heart is like a rainbow shell
    That paddles in a halcyon sea;
My heart is gladder than all these
    Because my love is come to me.

Raise me a dais of silk and down;
    Hang it with vair and purple dyes;
Carve it in doves and pomegranates,
    And peacocks with a hundred eyes:
Work it in gold and silver grapes,
    In leaves and silver fleurs-de-lys;
Because the birthday of my life
    Is come, my love is come to me.

Christina Rossetti 1830–94

Wedding Day

A man will leave his father and mother
and be united to his wife,
and the two will become one.

From the book of Genesis

God Gives You This Day

God gives you this day
This giggling day
As the clouds hokey-cokey
And the bride shines as new
And the angels remember
The wine that was water

God gives you this day
This glowfully day
Gift-wrapped in paradise
As the church whoops and chuckles
At the priest's proclamation
That one joined to one
In Christ, equals one

God gives you this day
This sanctified day
As He Who flicked stars
Fizzed this
Dressed, blessed,
Entirely-for-you-day
God gives you this day

Stewart Henderson

Being together

God created humankind in his image,
in the image of God he created them;
male and female he created them.

From the book of Genesis

Love Song

I see the pattern of stars and sun
And while they remain
You are fixed in my mind

And the course of the fox and the rabbit
A lad and his lady
The way of a woman with child.

While the waves run onto the beach
And the whale ploughs his road through the ocean
My love reaches out.

As long as the deer runs his race;
Until you can measure the edges of space
I will keep you.

Cathy Anderson

LOVE'S PASSION

Let him kiss me with the kisses of his mouth!
For your love is better than wine,
 your anointing oils are fragrant,
 your name is perfume poured out; . . .
As an apple tree among the trees of the wood,
 so is my beloved among young men.
With great delight I sat in his shadow,
 and his fruit was sweet to my taste.
He brought me to the banqueting house,
 and his intention toward me was love . . .

How fair and pleasant you are,
    O loved one, delectable maiden!
Oh may your breasts be like clusters of the vine,
    and the scent of your breath like apples,
and your kisses like the best wine
    that goes down smoothly,
        gliding over lips and teeth.

From the Song of Songs

LOVE'S FIDELITY

Be faithful to your own wife,
and give your love to her alone . . .
Be happy with your wife
and find your joy with the girl you married . . .
Why should you give your love to another woman, my son?
Why should you prefer the charms of another man's wife?

From the book of Proverbs

True Love

Let me not to the marriage of true minds
Admit impediments. Love is not love
Which alters when it alteration finds,
Or bends with the remover to remove: –
O no! it is an ever-fixed mark
That looks on tempests, and is never shaken;
It is the star to every wandering bark,
Whose worth's unknown,
   although his height be taken.
Love's not Time's fool, though rosy lips and cheeks
Within his bending sickle's compass come;
Love alters not with his brief hours and weeks,
But bears it out ev'n to the edge of doom.
If this be error, and upon me proved,
I never writ, nor no man ever loved.

William Shakespeare 1564–1616

Companionship

Two are better off than one, because they can work together more effectively. If one of them falls down, the other can help him up.

From the book of Ecclesiastes

Togetherness

Let there be spaces in your togetherness.
And let the winds of heaven dance between you.
Fill each other's cup but drink not from one cup.
Give one another of your bread but eat not from the same loaf.
Sing and dance together and be joyous, but let each one of you be alone,
Even as the strings of a lute are alone though they quiver with the same music.
And stand together yet not too near together:
For the pillars of the temple stand apart,
And the oak tree and the cypress grow not in each other's shadow.

Kahlil Gibran

LOVE'S GIVING

Love is patient and kind;
it is not jealous or conceited or proud;
love is not ill-mannered or selfish or irritable;
love does not keep a record of wrongs;
love is not happy with evil but is happy with the truth.
Love never gives up;
and its faith, hope, and patience never fail.

From the book of Corinthians

A Wife to a Husband

How do I love thee? Let me count the ways.
I love thee to the depth and breadth and height
My soul can reach, when feeling out of sight
For the end of Being and ideal Grace.
I love thee to the level of everyday's
Most quiet need, by sun and candlelight.
I love thee freely, as men strive for right;
I love thee purely, as they turn from praise.
I love thee with the passion put to use
In my old griefs, and with my childhood's faith.
I love thee with a love I seemed to lose
With my lost saints, – I love thee with the breath,
Smiles, tears, of all my life! – and, if God choose,
I shall but love thee better after death.

Elizabeth Barrett Browning 1806–61

LOVE AND TIME

Set me as a seal upon your heart,
 as a seal upon your arm;
for love is strong as death,
 passion fierce as the grave.
Its flashes are flashes of fire,
 a raging flame.
Many waters cannot quench love,
 neither can floods drown it.
If one offered for love
 all the wealth of his house,
it would be utterly scorned.

From the Song of Songs

A Marriage Ring

The ring so worn as you behold,
So thin, so pale, is yet of gold.
The passion such it was to prove
Worn with life's cares, love was yet love.

George Crabbe 1754–1832

Grow old along with me!
The best is yet to be,
The last of life for which the first was made.
Our times are in His hand
Who saith 'A whole I planned,'
Youth shows but half; trust God: see all,
nor be afraid.

Robert Browning 1812–99

BLESSINGS

May the Lord bless you and take care of you;
   May the Lord be kind and gracious to you;
May the Lord look on you with favour and
   give you peace.

From the book of Numbers

The eye of the great God be upon you,
The eye of the God of glory be on you,
The eye of the Son of Mary Virgin be on you,
The eye of the Spirit mild be on you,
To aid you and to shepherd you;
Oh the kindly eye of the Three be on you,
To aid you and to shepherd you.

Celtic Prayer

The Lord sanctify you and bless you,
The Lord pour the riches of his grace upon you,
that you may please him
and live together in holy love
to your lives' end.
So be it.

John Knox

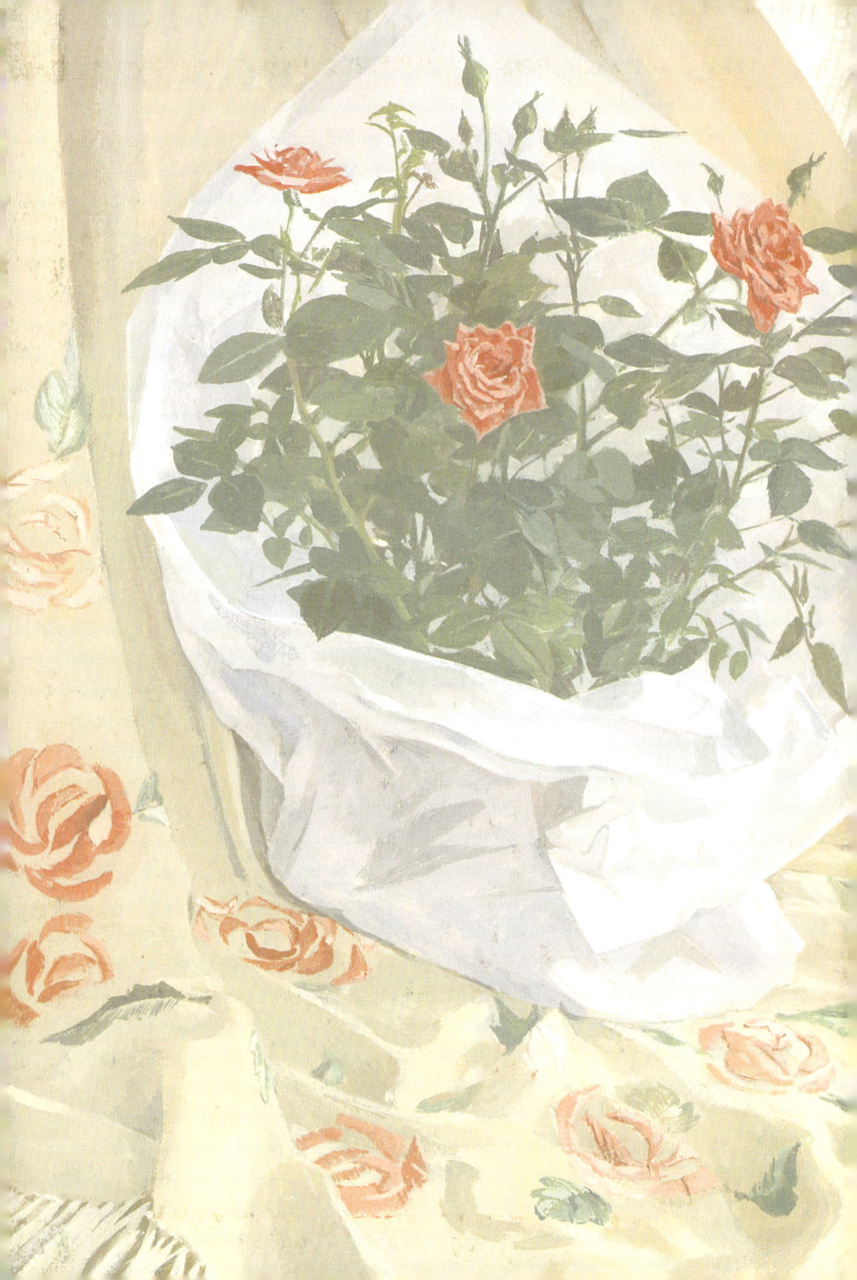